Textiles of Baluchistan

Textiles of Baluchistan
M.G. Konieczny

 Published for
The Trustees of The British Museum by
British Museum Publications Limited

© 1979 The Trustees of the British Museum
Illustrations © 1979 The Trustees of the British Museum,
except: figs. 2, 4–12, 14, 15, and plates 3, 40,
M G Konieczny; plates 33, 38, 41, 42, Museum für
Völkerkunde, Berlin.
ISBN 0 7141 1549 5 (paper)
ISBN 0 7141 1557 6 (cased)
Published by British Museum Publications Ltd
6 Bedford Square, London WC1B 3RA

British Library Cataloguing in Publication Data
Konieczny, M G
  Textiles of Baluchistan.
  1. Textile fabrics – Baluchistan   2. Museum
  of Mankind
  I. Title
  746'.09549'15   NK8876.7

Designed by Harry Green
Set in Monophoto Photina by Filmtype Services Limited,
Scarborough
Printed in Great Britain by Jarrold and Sons,
London and Norwich

Contents

List of Figures   *Page 6*

List of Plates   *7*

Foreword and Acknowledgements   *9*

The Baluchis and their textiles   *11*

Spinning   *13*

Dyeing   *13*

The loom   *16*

The weavers   *21*

Weaving   *22*

Tassels, fringes and other forms of ornamentation   *22*

Shells, bones and beads   *23*

Articles made and used in Central Baluchistan   *24*

Baluchi flat weave textiles in Sind and Derajat   *29*

Select Bibliography   *77*

List of Figures

Fig. 1   Map of Baluchistan
Fig. 2   Spindles
Fig. 3   Spindles
Fig. 4   Spindle whorls
Fig. 5   Plying, Chagai, Pakistan
Fig. 6   Spinning, Chagai, Pakistan
Fig. 7   The loom
Fig. 8   The position of the warp on the loom
            and shedding diagram of the loom
Fig. 9   Preparing leashes for the loom, Chagai, Pakistan
Fig. 10   Method of securing the warp beam, Sind, Pakistan
Fig. 11   Method of securing the breast beam, Chagai, Pakistan
Fig. 12   Supports for the heddle apparatus
Fig. 13   Comb beaters, Sind and Chagai, Pakistan
Fig. 14   Weaving, Sibi, Pakistan
Fig. 15   Weaving, Sind, Pakistan

List of Plates

1   Bedding cover, Chagai, Pakistan
2   Bedding cover, and detail, Chagai, Pakistan
3   Tent interior with bedding cover, Chagai, Pakistan
4   Floor cover, Kharan, Pakistan
5   Floor cover, Shorawak, south Afghanistan
6   Floor cover, Nimroz, Afghanistan
7   Floor cover, Nimroz, Afghanistan
8   Floor cover (detail), Sarawan, Pakistan
9   Floor cover, Mastung, Pakistan
10 Floor cover, Sind, Pakistan
11 Meal cloth, Nimroz, Afghanistan or Khorasan, Iran
12 Storage bag, Sind, Pakistan
13 Floor cover, Shorawak, south Afghanistan
14 Camel decoration, Dera Ismail Khan, Pakistan
15 Camel necklace, Chagai, Pakistan
16 Detail from a salt bag, Dalbandin, Pakistan
17 Floor cover, Las Bela, Pakistan
18 Storage bag, Chagai, Pakistan
19 Storage bag, Chagai, Pakistan
20 Detail from a floor cover, Sind, Pakistan
21 Floor cover, Dera Ismail Khan, Pakistan
22 Floor cover, Sind, Pakistan
23 Dough and bread bag, Chagai, Pakistan
24 Flour bags, Chagai, Pakistan
25 Runner, Chagai, Baluchistan
26 Storage bag, Chagai, Afghanistan
27 Saddle-bag, Khorasan, Iran or Herat, Afghanistan
28 Saddle-bag, Baluchistan, Iran
29 Saddle-bag, western Afghanistan
30 Koran bag, Chagai, Pakistan
31 Salt bag, Chagai, Pakistan
32 Salt bag, Chagai, Pakistan
33 Vanity bag, Chagai, Pakistan
34 Vanity bag, Nimroz, Afghanistan
35 Vanity bag, Nimroz, Afghanistan
36 Vanity bag, Nimroz, Afghanistan
37 Horse-shoe bag, Chagai or Sarawan, Pakistan
38 Horse nose-bag, Chagai, Pakistan
39 Camel saddle-cloth, Chagai, Pakistan
40 Camel wearing trappings, Chagai, Pakistan
41 Horse saddle cover, Chagai, Pakistan
42 Horse chest cover, Chagai, Pakistan
43 Greyhound cover, Chagai, Pakistan
44 Camel collar, Khorasan, Iran
45 Camel necklace, Afghanistan – Pakistan border
46 Net bag for dishes, Chagai, Pakistan
47 Cradle, Chagai, Pakistan
48 Prayer rug, Farah, Afghanistan

Numbers in the margins refer to Plates

Foreword and Acknowledgements

Since 1950 I have lived in Pakistan where until recently I was attached to the German Embassy as Director of the German Cultural Centre. Until 1968, I was also engaged in compiling a herpetological (reptile) collection from Pakistan for the Senckenberg Museum, Frankfurt am Main. In the course of touring the country for this herpetological field work I became interested in the traditional life of the inhabitants, and was especially attracted by the embroidery and textiles of the Baluchis. I therefore began to collect examples and detailed information about them. A part of this collection was exhibited by the Kunstamt (Arts Council) in Berlin — Reinickendorf in 1968 and afterwards acquired by the Abt. Westasien, Staatliche Museen (Preussischer Kulturbesitz) in Berlin — Dahlem. I wish to thank the Director of that Museum for allowing me to illustrate several pieces from that collection (plates 33, 38, 41 and 42). Other parts of my collection of textiles and embroideries were later acquired by the Museum of Mankind (the Ethnography Department of the British Museum), and by the Hamburgisches Museum für Völkerkunde, Hamburg. All of the textiles illustrated in this book, with the exception of those from the Berlin collection, are from the collection now in the Museum of Mankind.

I wish to express my deep thanks to the Government authorities who gave me great assistance in my work and to give special thanks to Khan Bahadur Sher Zaman Khan and to the many tribal chiefs for help and hospitality. Without the help of Nawabzadeh Abdulhamid Gichki, Nawabzadeh Jahan Jogezi, Sardar Omar Khan Sanjrani, Sardar Hashim Khan Sanjrani, Sardar Abdurrahman Khan Mengal and Mirbaz Khan Mengal I could not have collected the detailed information I sought. Gul Khan Nasir, the well-known poet of Nushki, has been kind enough to check my spelling of Baluchi technical terms, and J. G. S. Magson of the Halifax Museum has helped me with English weaving terminology. Last but not least I have to thank Shelagh Weir of the Museum of Mankind, British Museum, for editing my manuscript.

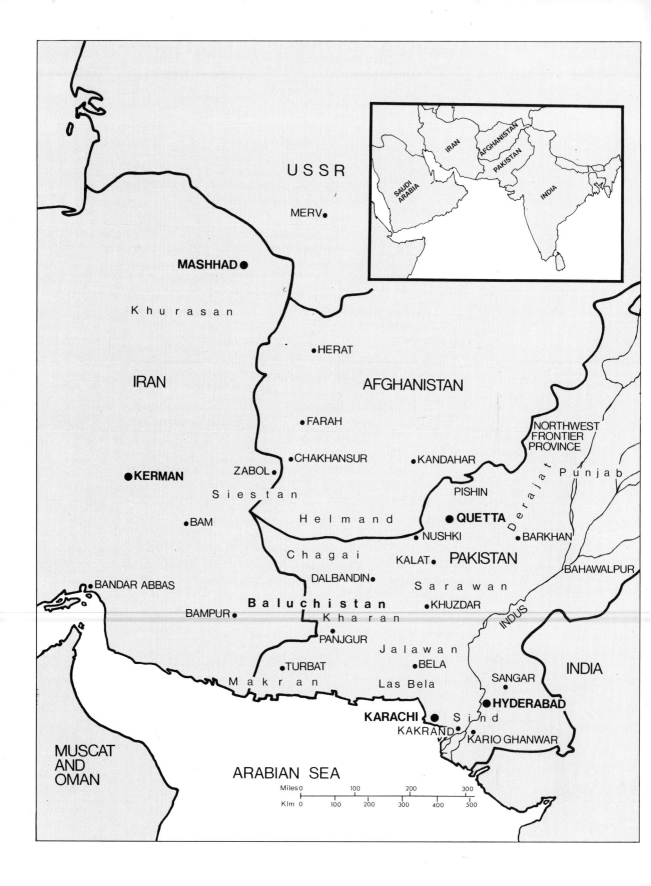

The Baluchis and their textiles

Today the Baluchis occupy the area bounded by Bandar Abbas and Bam in the west, the Punjab and the Kirthar range of mountains in the east, the Arabian Sea to the south, and areas of the Afghan province Chakhansur (Nimroz) and the Iranian province Seistan. There are large Baluch settlements in Sind, western Afghanistan, Khorasan and the Merv district. The land of the Baluchis is harsh and inhospitable, mostly deserts where raging sandstorms spring up suddenly, and small, impermanent streams burst into roaring torrents with the melting of the snow or occasional heavy rain. Much of this valuable water vanishes quickly into the parched plains and drought is frequent.

Records of the origins of the Baluchis are meagre but it is probable that over the centuries they have gradually migrated from the west and north-west. The Brahuis of Sarawan and Jhawalan speak a Dravidian language, and may represent the earliest inhabitants of the area. The Baluchis speak a language related to the eastern group of Iranian languages. Few large or enduring political groupings have ever existed in the area (the political organisation of the Mir Chakar Khan came to an end with his death), although the so-called Brahui Confederacy composed of the Khanat tribes of Kalat, Kharan, Makran and Las Bela existed in attenuated form under the name of the 'Baluchistan States Union' until the partition of 1947. During most of their history, however, the Baluchis have lived in smaller political units based on ties of kinship and locality.

About 60 per cent of Baluchis still lead a nomadic life. They subsist on milk products from their goats and sheep, dates, the fruit of the wild dwarf palm, wild pistacio nuts, vegetables and melons, dried mulberries, and at times of extreme hardship, on wild flowers and plants. The precarious nature of their existence is reflected in a proverb referring to periods of famine: 'their hands are on the wild plants and their eyes are on the stars' (looking for rain). At such times in the past the Baluchis were driven by starvation to raid the settlements of their more prosperous neighbours. This frequently led to severe reprisals although their enemies never managed to conquer them. Their fierce independence and capacity for survival has secured them a reputation for endurance and heroism.

The possessions of the nomadic Baluchis are few and simple: their homes are goat-hair tents or huts of palm fronds and brush or wickerwork, or of tamarisk branches; they drink water from a folded dwarf palm leaf; they make fire by twirling a stick in a notched piece of wood; and they bake bread by simple methods such as wrapping the dough round a heated stone placed adjacent to the embers of the fire. Their few tools and domestic utensils are provided by the Luris who have long been their bards, armourers and craftsmen, or were, until the partition with India, bought from Hindu tradesmen in nearby towns. The intricacy and beauty of the embroidery and

11

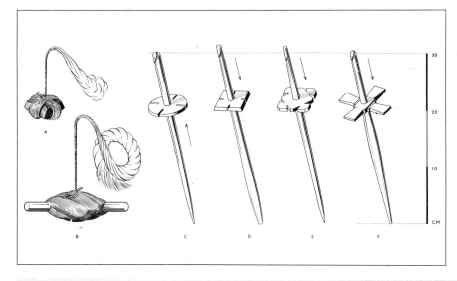

Fig. 2 Spinning elements used by Baluchis
A Stone or piece of hard clay. Las Bela and Sind, Pakistan
B Short stick which is rotated horizontally. Jhalawan, Las Bela and Sind, Pakistan
C Wood spindle with circular whorl with slits for catching the spun thread. Chakhansur, Afghanistan and Chagai, Pakistan
D Spindle with square whorl with slits for catching spun thread. Kharan, Pakistan
E Spindle with square whorl with cut-outs. Awaran, Jhalawan, Pakistan
F Spindle with whorl formed by two crossed pieces of wood. Chagai, Pakistan

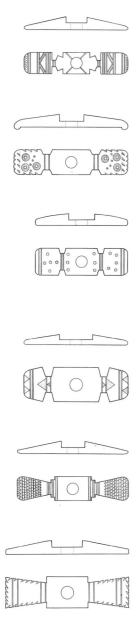

Fig. 4 Designs carved on wooden cross pieces of spindle whorls, Pakistan.

Fig. 3 *Left* Stone used as spindle weight, with pin used to secure yarn.   1972 AS2 93
Right Wooden spindles with whorls formed by two crossed pieces of wood.   1972 AS2 15, 16 & 17 and 1972 AS7 18.

the textiles produced by the Baluchi women therefore provide a striking contrast to the simplicity of the rest of their material culture. This book is concerned with describing the methods of manufacture of the traditional flat woven textiles of the Baluchis.

Spinning

The simplest spinning implements used are weights made from any material to hand. In Las Bela and Jhalawan a stone weight is used, and in the stoneless plain of Sind a lump of sun-dried clay the size of a chicken's egg. In the same areas a stick (*dērō*) is also used which rotates in the horizontal plane. The most commonly used spinning implement used by the Baluchis is, however, a spindle (*jallak*) with a vertical wooden shaft and a wooden whorl in one of three main forms — a notched disc, a notched square or simple crossed sticks.

Spinning is done by men, women or children. Usually the raw wool is left unwashed and is teased by hand without any special implement (although the Baluchis in Khorasan and Herat use a carding comb). A rove is drawn out from the mass of wool, wound round the left forearm and wrist and held in the left hand. A finer length of about 30 cm. is then drawn from the rove by the right hand, twisting it at the same time, and the end is attached to the spindle or weight as described above. This length is that from which the spun thread is to be made. The left hand is lifted so that the spindle or weight is suspended, and the latter is twirled by the right hand so as to spin the thread. As the spinning proceeds, more wool is drawn out of the prepared rove. The spun thread is then wound round the spindle or weight, and the process is repeated. The thread is secured on the latter by a thorn or splinter of wood. On the spindle, the spun thread is wound round the shaft below the whorl, passed through a notch or between the cross pieces of the whorl, as the case may be, wound round the shaft above the whorl, and caught in a notch at the top of the shaft. Sometimes the spinner works sitting, first twirling the spindle clockwise on the ground like a top, then lifting it so that it rotates suspended from the twisted wool. The spun thread is then unhooked, stretched and wound onto the spindle shaft by turning the latter anti-clockwise. Alternatively the spinner spins while standing or walking (shepherds might spin thus while following their flocks), rotating the spindle by twisting the lower end of the shaft. In this case the spin will be anti-clockwise. Another method, employed by old people, is to roll the spindle with the palm of the hand from the thigh to the knee. The thread is spun in an anti-clockwise direction by this method. After spinning the yarn is wound off the spindle or weight into balls weighing up to two kilograms.

Dyeing

Undyed yarn alone is used by tribes or individuals who are too poor to obtain artificial dyestuffs or who are a long way from the markets where they can be bought. Nevertheless undyed wools still provide a considerable range of shades for weaving, for example the wool of the dromedary ranges in colour from white and light yellow to dark brown, sheep's wool provides white yarn (and in southern Sind, brown) and black or grey hair can be obtained from the goat. To this range of natural colours such poor or isolated groups occasionally add a few threads of bartered red yarn. Most

13

Fig. 5 Boy plying yarn by drawing thread simultaneously from two balls. The two threads are tied to a stone which is circled first around the head and then around the body, while the threads are drawn from the balls. When 4–5 metres have been plyed, it is wound round the stone, fastened with a pin, and the process repeated. Dalbandin, Chagai, Pakistan.

Fig. 6 Woman unwinding a length of spun thread from the upper spindle shaft (after spinning in the sitting position with the spindle suspended). Photographed at a camp near the entrance to the pass leading to the shrine of Sheikh Hussein, Rast Koh, Chagai, Pakistan.

Baluchis, however, employ a wide range of coloured yarns in their textiles.

Dyeing was, and still is, carried out by professional (male) craftsmen in various towns, but in more remote areas dyeing has remained the responsibility of the women who use a variety of pigments derived from wild plants. The general use of such natural dyes began to decline about a century ago with the introduction of imported chemical (aniline) dyes (*jauhar*) which entered the area through Bombay, Karachi, Shikarpur and Quetta. These dyes came mainly from Germany, though they sometimes appear in statistical returns as 'Belgian' because they were shipped through Antwerp. The chemical dyes seem to have been accepted first by the dyers of Quetta who used them for cotton as well as wool. Later their use gradually spread among those living in or near the caravan trails. The spread of chemical dyes caused a decline in the cultivation of local dye plants. After 1900 the madder fields in Sarawan, and the indigo fields of Dadhar (Kachhi), Sibi and Bam dwindled rapidly and soon disappeared altogether, despite the former widespread fame of the dyes produced in these regions. Madder, for example, had been exported previously to Sind and Punjab, and indigo to Central Asia (Minchin, 1907, p. 99 and Morris, 1884, pp. 161–66).

The following are the dyes used to achieve the various colours found in Baluch woven textiles. The Baluch term is given first, if known, followed by the botanical name.

RED: root of madder (*majīt* = *Rubia tinctorium*); bark of rhamnus (*Rhamnus persicus*); bark of jujube (*Zizyphus nummularia*), and rhubarb roots (*rēwand* = *Rheum*).

ORANGE: the material was first dyed with madder and dipped into a decoction of crushed pomegranate husks (*anār* = *Punica granatum*), or of poplar leaves (*padag* = *Populus euphratica*), or willow leaves (*gēt* = *Salix*).

YELLOW: Turmeric (*dar-e-zard, zard chōb* = the rhizomes of *Curcuma longa*); flowers of sophora (*Sophora griffithii*); flowers of safflower (*kajūr, kajīra* = *Carthamus tinctorius*); flower-petals of delphinium (*eshwarg, zalīl* = *Delphinium zalil*); galls of prosopis (*zangōwach* = *Prosopis stephaniana*); stems of ephedra (*khoshk targ* = *Ephedra pachyclada*); fresh stems of artemisia (*dranag* = *Artemisia*); leaves of apricot trees (*zardālū* = *Prunus armeniaca*); willow (*gēt* = *Salix*); apple trees (*sēb* = *Pyrus*); wild pistacio trees (*gwan* = *Pistacia terebinthus*, var. *mutica*), and other wild plants according to experience.

GREEN: the material was first dyed with indigo and then dipped into a boiling solution of yellow dyestuffs such as turmeric (*Curcuma longa*), leaves of apricot (*Prunus armeniaca*) or willow trees (*Salix*), fresh branches of saxaol (*tā-gaz* = *Haloxylon ammodendron*), or flowers of sophora (*Sophora griffithii*).

BLUE: indigo (*nīl* = *Indigofera tinctoria*).

VIOLET: after having been dyed with madder, the material was soaked in indigo solution.

BROWN AND BLACK: pomegranate skins (*Punica granatum*); leaves of wild pistacio trees (*Pistacia terebinthus*, var. *mutica*), or walnut bark (*joz* = *Juglans regia*) in combination with *mak* (see below) were used (see Gupte, 1907, pp. 198–99; Hughes, 1907, pp. 131–33; Masson, 1844, pp. 440–41, and Minchin, 1907, pp. 115–16).

MORDANTS: the mordants employed in dyeing were and are *mak* (*phulmak, khāgal* or *zāgh*), a ferrous sulphate with impurities of silica alumina, and lime (mainly mined in Jhalawan and Koh-e-Chihiltan, Taftan) (see Minchin, 1907, pp. 160–61), and *khār*, a crude carbonate of soda, which is actually the solidified sap that has been extracted by a heating process from saltwort bushes (*shōrag* = *Salsola foetida, S. griffithii, Suaeda fruticosa*, and other species), mixed with date juice (*gūr*), alum or lime.

The Loom

The Baluchis, like many other nomadic peoples, weave on a horizontal ground-loom. Their looms are constructed from simple local materials and there are no specialist loom-makers. Straight branches or lengths of imported bamboo serve as beams, palm branches or strong reed stems (*nāl* = *Phragmites communis*) are used for the rods, and the ropes and cords are made from wool, goat hair or fibres derived from the leaf of the dwarf palm. A length of metal piping which the weaver might find by chance can also be used for one of the beams.

The warping is done between the warp and breast beams set some distance apart, and placed for this purpose on two piles of stones. The warp thread is passed alternately under and over these beams so as to cross over between them. To obtain a strong selvedge they use a warp which has up to eight 2-ply strands, or several plaited strands. The length and width of the warp threads depends on the size of the article to be woven and the time at the weaver's disposal. If the work cannot be completed during the period between setting up one camp, and moving to the next, the width woven will generally be under 90 cm. as a loom of this size is easier to roll up (complete with its wooden components), and fasten to the back of a pack animal. When it is necessary to produce a larger piece of cloth, for example a floor cover, two widths of cloth are woven and sewn together lengthways. Larger widths are only woven at the fixed summer and winter camps or when a tribe has set up a permanent settlement. The longest warps used are those for weaving curtains (*shaffī*) which are rarely more than six metres long. However I encountered warps thirteen metres long at Hassu Goth near the Rungani river and at Munshi Saleh Muhammad Goth in the Haro Range (Las Bela). On this three Angaria women were weaving no less than four floor covers (*zīl*) successively. Such an extraordinary loom would usually present grave problems for it is difficult to keep the warp in tension over such a length. In this case the women worked in the cool early morning when the 80–90 per cent humidity kept the warps stretched tight. (The usual high humidity of this area, which is only five kilometres from the sea, may be one of the reasons why Angaria-woven cloth has a looser texture than that woven in the far drier areas of the rest of Baluchistan where humidity is about 5–10 per cent.)

Once the warping is completed, the shed-stick (*padā-e-gul-e-dār*) is pulled through the shed on the far side of the 'crossing' from the weaver, and the heddle-rod (*demā-e-gul-e-dār*) is placed over the warp threads on the weaver's side of the 'crossing' and alternate warp threads are tied to it with leashes. Leashes of equal length are obtained by placing the handle of the beater over the heddle-rod, and winding the leashes round both. Afterwards the beater handle is removed. The warp is then stretched to the correct tension by, first, placing the breast beam over pegs in the ground, then lashing the warp beam to pegs in the ground 1 to 1.5 metres away from it. A tripod, with a horizontal bar tied across the two legs facing the weaver, is then set

Fig. 7 The loom used by Baluchi nomads, with tripod supporting the heddle apparatus.

Fig. 8 Diagram to show (a) the position of the warp threads on the Baluch loom, and (b) the formation of the shed and countershed.

A warp beam   (*sar pōkhtu*)
B breast beam   (*pād pōkhtu*)
C odd threads   (*shatt*)
D even threads   (*shatt*)
E shed-stick (*padā-e gul-e dār*)
F string round upper warp (*winda*)
G heddle-rod (*demā-e gul-e dār*)
H leash   (*gulag*)
I heading string, with spiral leashes around the cloth beam (*winda*)
J peg   (*mēkh*)
K tension rope   (*sar kash*)
L tripod   (*trikar*)
M support for rocker   (*bārdār*)
N rocker   (*makrī*)
O shed
P countershed
Q fabric   (*guāfta*)
R temple   (*panād kash*)

16

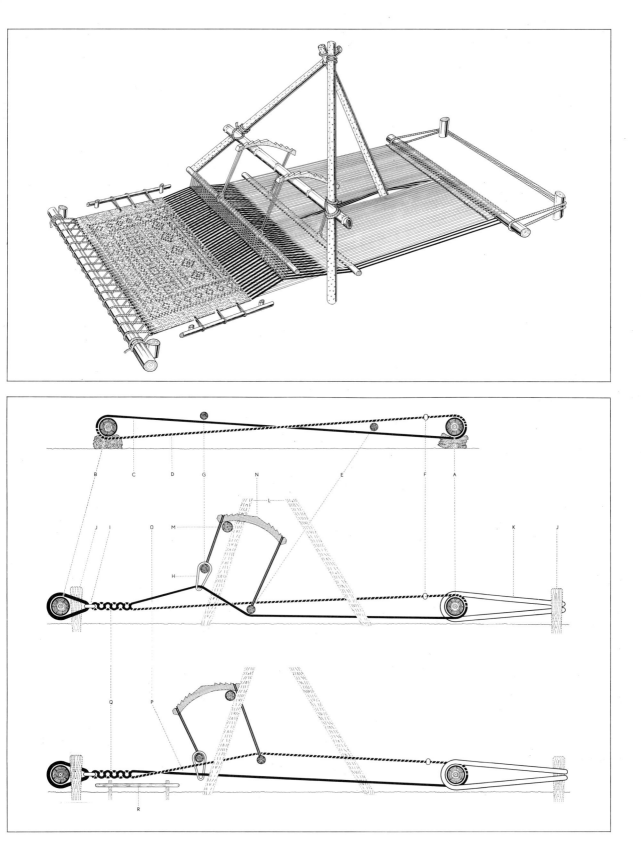

Fig. 9 Woman attaching the leashes to the heddle-rod, using the handle of a comb beater to space them. Dalbandin, Chagai, Pakistan.

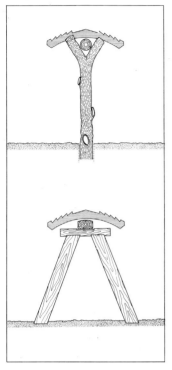

Fig. 11 Method of securing the breast beam. Note also the method for maintaining widthways tension. The article being woven is a flour bag. Dalbandin, Chagai, Pakistan.

Fig. 12 Two alternative methods of supporting each end of the rod on which the rocker rests. Used by Baluchis who have settled permanently in the Indus valley. *Above* forked branch, Kakrand, Mirpur Sakro, Sind, Pakistan. *Below* trestle, Kario Ganwhar, Sind, Pakistan.

up over the warp threads. The height of this bar is between 60–75 cm. from the ground. One or two rockers (*makrī*), depending on the width of the warp threads, are placed across this bar, and one end of each rocker is attached by a cord to the shed-stick, and the other end to the heddle-rod. During weaving alternate warp threads are raised by pushing down or lifting up the end of the rocker nearest the weaver. The tripod and heddle apparatus is moved along the length of the loom as the weaving progresses. Before and during weaving the tension of the warp threads can be adjusted as necessary by twisting the tension ropes with a pin, adjusting the tripod legs closer or further apart, and moving the cords on the rockers to different notches. Increase in tension is also gained by the weight of the weaver sitting on the part she has completed. In order to achieve an evenly tensioned fabric and straight selvedges a system of cross-tensioning is also used. This is done by driving a pair of pegs into the ground about 60–90 cm. apart and about 20–30 cm. away from each selvedge. A stick is placed behind each of these, parallel with the warp threads, and three or four cords are led round these sticks, through the selvedges of the woven fabric and tightened. Widthways tension is increased by pushing a stick or peg through the cords and twisting it. These stretchers are moved along the loom, like the heddle apparatus, as weaving progresses.

The Baluchis usually weave in the open air and build a shelter of old mats, blankets or branches to protect themselves from the burning heat of the sun. Only in a few places in Sind (for example, Kario Ganwhar) are looms set up inside the huts. When the loom is set up in the open, and there is a danger that unpenned sheep and goats may walk into it during the night, the tension ropes attached to the warp beam are loosened at the end of the day's work and then re-tensioned next morning.

In the areas where Baluchis have founded permanent settlements (in Sind, Punjab and Bahawalpur) they have adopted loom apparatus more characteristic of settled people. Instead of the light tripod, so conveniently folded and packed for travelling, the looms in these areas have trestles (*gōrī*) (in Kario Ganwhar) and pairs of forked branches (in Kakrand) to support the beam on which the rockers pivot back and forth. Trestles can be moved along the loom in the same way as the tripod, but the branches are inserted into holes in the ground at intervals along the length of the loom and can be shifted only to a fixed series of positions.

The Weavers

In the past it was customary to train young girls in the craft of weaving and a bride-to-be was always eager to produce as much of her trousseau as she could in this way. However, in the last few decades fewer girls have learned the craft. Now a girl who wants a particular woven cloth for her marriage has to buy it second-hand, acquire it by barter, or commission it from an older woman. Some of these women are aware of their special skills and refuse to tolerate an assistant working with them, claiming they would spoil the quality of their weaving. In this way the art of weaving is being lost forever.

Weavers are not paid fixed sums for their work but are provided with their two daily meals, tea and pocket money. The reputations of elderly women who are specially skilled in weaving may stretch far beyond the borders of their tribe and endure even after their death. In Lunah, Dubbah

Buttan, Katawari and Kandewari in the Haro Range, I was told many times that a floor cover (*zīl*) of which I showed a photograph could, because of its pattern, only have been produced by either Tajan or Mote, two women who had died about forty years previously. Only in the Kethrani tribe are the weavers always male. In the other tribes the weavers are almost exclusively women, although one hears about, and occasionally encounters, men who also know and practise the craft. I met a male weaver, near Dalbandin, weaving some tent cloth, who claimed he was also familiar with the art of flat weaving.

Weaving

The Baluchis use no plans or sketches in planning the patterns for a woven article. The weaver usually keeps in her mind the pattern she has learned to weave and which she wishes to create, although sometimes a weaver will keep an old fragment of cloth from which to copy designs. When two or more women are weaving together on the same loom they agree beforehand what patterns they will use. Once they have begun, however, they may still alter their ideas about the form of the decorative border stripes (*harīr*) along the selvedge and may narrow or widen these as the work progresses. From such alterations one can sometimes work out the point where a piece of weaving was recommenced after a break. The yarn used for the weft may be a single or doubled thread. The weft is passed by hand through the shed or countershed created by raising and lowering the shed-stick and heddle-rod alternately. Usually no special implement is used to pass the weft through (a 'pick') and the yarn is simply pulled through by hand. An exception to this is in Las Bela where the Angaria women use a stick spool consisting of a slab of wood 50–60 cm. long and 3–4 cm. wide around which the weft thread is wound. The shed and countershed were formed by alternately raising and lowering the shed-stick and heddle-rod by pushing down or lifting up the rockers to which they are attached by cords. The upper and lower warp threads are not completely separated by this action as their rough texture causes them to stick together, and the weaver has to run the fingers of both hands back and forth from side to side to separate them completely. The upper threads are supported by the forearm and hand of one arm while the pick is made with the other. When a design is being woven by the floating weft technique, the requisite warp threads are selected with the one hand and the pick is made with the other. The weft is beaten in after every pick with a comb beater similar to those used on vertical pile-carpet looms in the Middle East, but it has less teeth – only five – and the teeth and handle are longer. The greater length of the Baluchi beater relates to the fact that it is used more as a lever than a beater in forcing the weft threads tightly together.

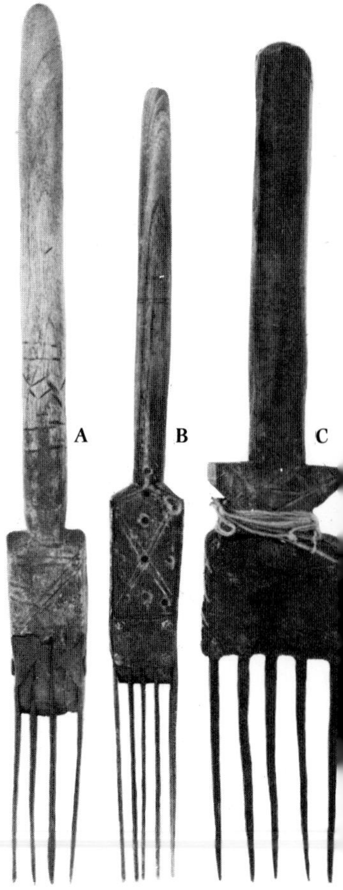

Fig. 13 Comb beaters. **A**: Sind, Pakistan. **B** and **C**: Chagai, Pakistan. 1972 AS2 11–13.

Tassels, fringes and other forms of ornamentation

Tassels (*phul*) are directly fixed onto the various articles by passing the thread back and forth through the edge of the fabric until a skein of required length and thickness has been made. For binding the skein, a strong thin cord is attached to it near the edge of the article, slung around the big toe and bound round the skein by turning the latter in the hands. This binding is plain or can be decorated all round with a herringbone or lozenge-like pattern, called the 'wild ass eye' (*gōr chashm*). For this purpose coloured

22

threads are fixed to the thin cord at the top of the skein, left hanging down the skein, and wound around the cord whenever required for the pattern. Much practice is needed to make this beautiful decoration, the most perfect specimens of which are found on old tassels. Experts in this technique enjoy a far reaching reputation. In Khorasan and Afghanistan the Baluchis attach short bulky skeins of wool instead of precisely made tassels.

Bags for medicinal earth, salt and valuables are adorned with pendant tassels, that is three additional tassels hanging on plaited cords from the main tassel described above. Such pendants – usually also decorated with cowrie-shells – are called *chughur phul*. Sometimes pieces of tubular bones from sheep or goat, green or blue coloured glass beads from Herat or turquoise glazed clay beads from Kerman are threaded on the cords. Bags which are also used as runners (*dasdān, jamdān* and *pōnchī*) are decorated with pendants of small tassels, five, seven, nine or more, each one set closely above the other (*lārō*). These tassels are decorated with marzinella shells, and usually made of silk.

Rosettes ingeniously worked from floss silk in different colours, and ornamented with marzinella shells, are sometimes used on ornamental covers for animals (*jhul*). Floor covers are hemmed or given fringes made from the loose warp ends which are sometimes knotted or plaited. On bedding covers (*shaffī*) several warp threads at each end of the fabric are plaited to make tapes. Two or three of these are then joined to nooses with which the cover is fastened vertically. The bed covers (*katpōsh*) sometimes have carefully worked fringes made by plaiting several warp threads to cords which are then joined to a fret-like arrangement with small tassels at the ends. Loop fringes are added all around to ornamental covers for animals (*jhul*) by pulling yarns of various colours through the edges, and winding them around a stick which is afterwards removed. According to the number of shades, the fringes are called 'three', 'five' or 'seven flower' (*phul*). Bags are occasionally given rows of short loop fringes or long fringes across the central panel while they are woven, as mentioned in the section on weaving.

White, coloured silk, silver and gold threads (*gulābatūn*) were once used by the Maddat-Khani tribe of Khorasan (Iran) and the Reki and Rakhshani tribes of Nimroz, Afghanistan, in their weaving. I have seen pieces at least 150 years old in the homes of tribal chiefs in which metal threads were used instead of white or yellow.

Shells, bones and beads
Baluch textiles are often ornamented with shells from the Arabian Sea.

The cowrie shell (*kuchk = Cypraea turdus*, 20–40 mm.), is used mainly on the cords of hanging tassels (*chughur phul*). A large hole is made through the back of the whorl and the shell is then fixed with goat-hair thread through the upper and lower end so that the aperture is visible.

The moon shell (*zangūlag = Polynices mammilla*, 20–35 mm.) is used in close-set rows to border the edges of the storage-bag (*takkī*). This shell is also used for decorating one long edge of bags or runners such as *dasdān, jamdān* and *pōnchī*. A hole is pierced through the last whorl for the thread and the shell is secured in such a manner that the intact part of its whorl is visible.

The olive shell (*gōsh-dard = Oliva*, 20–40 mm.), is applied like the moon shell, but the hole is made at its apex by breaking or grinding.

The marzinella shell (*duttuk kuchk* = *Marzinella*, 5–10 mm.), is pierced on the left side of the aperture near the apex for the thread. This tiny species is used for adorning small tassels (*lārō*) and occasionally for decorating embroideries.

Besides shells, pieces of tubular bone from fowl, sheep or goat, cut to a length of from 1–3 cm., are occasionally threaded on the cords of hanging tassels (*chughur phul*). They are not as durable as the stronger shells and eventually break off.

In addition to or instead of these natural products green or blue coloured glass beads from Herat and turquoise glazed clay beads from Kerman are used.

Articles made and used in Central Baluchistan

At the height of the development of this nomadic art a number of very fine articles were produced and used. Of these the *shaffī* was undoubtedly the finest. The Baluchis use this term exclusively for a curtain with which they cover the bedding, blankets, quilts and cushions which they stack on a wooden trestle (*partal*) or on the floor at one end of the tent or hut. The most attractive feature of a *shaffī* is a border (*harīr*) running the length of the fabric on one or both sides and transversing the pattern stripes. When woven in white wool this gives the impression of white lace. Next to the *shaffī* in quality is the *kōnt*, which is used as a floor cover. Since for practical reasons the width of the loom is limited, a broad *kōnt* is sometimes made up from two loom widths with stripes woven so as to correspond. Skilled weavers frame the *kōnt* with a border in the floating weft technique similar to the above mentioned *harīr*, but with less elaborate patterns. In specimens from Seistan and Chakhansur (Nimroz) white embroidery is sometimes substituted for this border. The Baluchis of Sind call this floor cover *falasī* or *farasī*, and the Angaria of Las Bela, *zīl*. These terms are used for pieces with pattern stripes, while those with plain coloured stripes are called *garrag* (Baluchi) or *kharrarī* (by the Baluchis in Sind). In the tent this floor cover is spread out next to the *shaffī*, and marks the place where the head of the family sits. It is also the place where a respected guest is requested to take his seat, and where the *hāl* – the customary enquiries about the visitor's well-being and his news – are made. If the guest is staying for a short while, refreshments such as water, yoghurt, dates, and perhaps a meal are offered to him at this place. The meal is served on the *parzōnag*, a square or rectangular meal cloth with one tassel at each corner. The bread is brought wrapped in the *shēken* (*bēshenk*), a bag in which the dough, and after baking the flat loaves, are kept warm. This bag (approximately one metre square) usually has a broad band on each side containing several pattern stripes. Such a bag can be recognised by the manner in which it is finished. The selvedges are stitched together only halfway so that the upper half of the bag can be turned over like a flap to allow the bread to be placed inside more easily. The flap is then folded back and the sides of the *shēken* are folded inwards, the various layers of the fabric giving excellent insulation. A tassel is fixed to the lower corners.

For a comfortable rest a bed cover (*katpōsh*) is provided. It resembles the *kōnt* but is not as broad and the fringes are often joined in a fret-like manner. This bed cover is either put directly on the ground or over a bedstead (*kat*).

Cereals are stored in sacks (*gowālag*) similar in size to those common in

Fig. 14 Woman weaving a bedding cover. Bagh, Kachhi, Sibi, Pakistan.

24

western countries, or larger. A peculiarity of grain bags is the predominant use of goat hair for warp as well as weft, and the loose weave which allows for the aeration of the grain. Flour bags of medium size are also called *gowālag*, while the small size is called *tūrag*, a term that is used for the horse nose-bag as well. Flour bags are tightly woven with sheep wool. Double corn sacks (*ghindī* or *ghundī*) are produced in the north-eastern part of the country. They are made from two large bags which are sewn together lengthwise and placed on the pack-animal like a pair of saddle-bags. The mouth of the *ghindī* is shaped like a bottleneck, so that it can be closed easily and safely.

Fig. 15 Two young women weaving a floor cover (*khararī*), Kakrand, Sind, Pakistan. (This loom is now in the Museum of Mankind: 1972 AS2 5).

The top of the bedding pile is covered with runners (*dasdān*) or rectangular bags (*jamdān*) which are produced by folding a *dasdān*. Moon shells are sewn in a line to one of the long sides, and at least three tassels are attached to the same edge so that they hang down over the upper part of the vertically stretched *shaffī*. The *jamdān* is used by some people as a cushion, although the original Persian word means 'storage bag'. [25][26]

Clothes and utensils are kept in storage bags (*takkī* or *bālisht* when used as a cushion) which are always made in pairs to facilitate an equal loading on pack-animals. Two sizes are generally in use, a rectangular type, and in Jhalawan and Las Bela, a square type. The *takkī* is often decorated with a line of moon shells along the bottom edge and one long edge which becomes the bottom edge when loaded on an animal. The square type has, in addition to the shell decoration, two extremely long and heavy tassels on both sides of the opening. These bags are closed with a cord which is pulled through loops just inside the opening of the bag. Sometimes a rectangular *takkī* is fastened on a camel to carry a sick child, sheep or goat. When used in this way the *takkī* is the equivalent of the once widespread saddle-bag (*khōrjīn*, *hōrjīn*) which served mainly for carrying the necessities of life for people travelling on donkey or horseback. [12][18][19][27][28][29]

The original length of the cloth for a saddle-bag is approximately $4\frac{1}{2}$ times that of the width, plus a stripe in the warp direction on both selvedges and one side to strengthen the finished article. A square at each end contains a panel with the favourite pattern of the tribe. The panel is surrounded by one or more borders. The other part of the cloth (which forms the back of the completed *hōrjīn*) usually has plain coloured stripes. Only rare old specimens have pattern stripes here. Both ends with their panels are turned over – the right side up – for shaping the pair of pockets, and the selvedges are stitched together by oversewing them with goat-hair thread. Vertical slits are left in the horizontal stripe above the panel, and strong goat-hair loops are attached to the opposite side for closing the bags. These loops are pulled one by one through the slits and through each other, and the last one is tied or sealed if the contents are confidential. Since horses have become rare in central Baluchistan, horse saddle-bags are hardly ever seen today. Other articles found in the tent or used for travel are smaller bags in which objects of high status, value or practical importance are kept. They have distinctive shapes and fittings according to their purpose (which may help in the more precise identification of analogous bags in the pile technique). When in camp they are hung in the black tent giving a decorative and attractive effect. While travelling they are often carried hanging over the shoulder. Some bags are no longer needed since customs have changed, but their names are still used, sometimes inaccurately, today.

The Koran bag (*Qur'ānjal*) is meant only for the protection of the Holy Book. It is square in shape with a tribal pattern woven in a square panel surrounded by borders with horizontal stripes above it. While weaving two vertical slits are left on both sides of the upper border stripe and a plaited tape in two colours is passed through them for closing it. It has one tassel on each corner and a fifth in the centre of the lower edge. The design is the same on both sides. When it is kept in a tent or hut it is hung in the *qiblah* direction (towards Mecca). [30]

The salt bag (*wādān*) serves for keeping rock salt or salt that has been collected from the deposits of a *hamūn* (salt waste). It is shaped like a geo- [31][32]

metrical bottle and the mouth resembles that of the corn sack (*ghindī*). At the top a plaited cord is attached to both corners for hanging it up. It has the same designs on each side and is decorated with seven sets of tassels. Similar to the salt bag is the *chamchadān*, a bag in which spoons (*chamcha*) are kept. Its mouth is broader than the salt bag.

The bag for healing earth (*khōrdajal, hōrdajal*) is used for keeping dust or mud that has been collected from the area surrounding the grave or shrine of a saintly woman or man. This earth, mostly consisting of diluvial and alkaline substances, is used for the same purposes as various types of healing earth (Fuller's earth) are used today in the western world — externally for the treatment of bruises, tumefaction, rheumatism, etc., and orally for the adjustment of stomach and intestinal disorders. The fabric of the *khōrdajal* is extremely fine but the panel, filled with a clear, rich repeat pattern, is hardly visible because of the many tassels (*chughur phul*) which are not only attached to the edges but also along the border of the opening, thus covering most of the intricate and beautiful design. A plaited cord is attached for hanging.

The *khōrdajal* is sometimes used as a vanity bag, in which case it is called *istrajal* (*istrag* = razor). This name is also applied to a small and richly
33 embroidered bag that is made from a square piece of material (approxi-
34 mately 30 × 30 cm.) by folding three corners into the centre, sewing them,
35 and using the fourth corner as a flap for closing it. This was originally the
36 book cover so common in Muslim countries for the safe-keeping of the Koran. Some people also call the *khōrdajal khīsajal*. But this name was used originally for bags in which gunpowder was carried (*khīsag* = gunpowder) in the days when it was needed for matchlock guns.

The horse-shoe bag (*nāldān*), once an important requisite for a horseman,
37 has vanished with the decrease in horse breeding and the consequent disappearance of horses in many areas. They are generally smaller in size than the bags described above, decorated with five or seven tassels (*phul*), one on each corner, and one in the centre of the lower edge, and occasionally one on each top edge. This bag also has a plaited cord fixed to the edges of the opening for hanging. It can easily be differentiated from other bags by the small narrow loops used to close it, in order to prevent the horse-shoe nails dropping out. Instead of *nāldān* I have heard the name distorted into words like *dāldān, lāldān* and *nārdān*.

The ration bag (*chintag*) is still in common use among shepherds. Old specimens are woven with black goat hair and white sheep wool. They have a plaited cord or band as a shoulder strap, and an individual tassel (*phul*) is attached to the lower corners. Hessian cloth is now being used increasingly for ration bags.

The horse nose-bag (*tūrag*, Pers, *tubra*) is similar in size to the Koran bag
38 but has no slits for the tape. Instead the plaited tape is fixed to the corners of the opening. To each of these corners a hanging tassel (*chughur phul*) is also attached, and another tassel (*phul*) is fixed to the middle of the tape as shown in Plate 38.

The money bag (*pēlag*) is the smallest of all the bags. It does not exceed one hand-span in length or two-thirds in width, but square-shaped wallets were also produced. Since it was carried in one of the inner side pockets of the shirt, it was woven with finest yarn to ensure the greatest flexibility of texture. The yarn was spun preferably from the fine hair of the goat's fleece (*kurk*). It has dainty patterns, is decorated with two or three tassels (*phul*)

28

at the lower edge, two tassels on the upper edges, and has a cord attached to one of the edges which is wound round the bag to close it. This type of bag was occasionally used for keeping tobacco and consequently named *tambakdān*. Other names used for it are *bukhchā* and, in Sind, *būchhān*. If bags for money or tobacco are required today they are produced in embroidery.

Another group of textiles comprises saddle cloths for riding animals and ornamental covers for cattle (*jhul*). Their general layout resembles that of the floor cover (*kŏnt*) with or without a border round the panel, but in some of them an extra panel is set in the centre. Either type of tassel (*phul* or *chughur phul*) or loop fringes are attached all round the edges. It seems that their characteristic layout has been preserved in some of the so-called *farasī* textiles. Of the undermentioned types, no. 1 can still often be found, no. 2 is rarely found, and nos. 3 and 4 have completely disappeared.

1. A saddle-cloth for dromedaries (*ushter-e-jhul*) which has a rectangular 39 cutout in the centre for the hump. The shape of this *jhul* is more or less 40 rectangular, corresponding to its use for single or double saddles.

2. A roughly square-shaped saddle-cloth for horses (*asp-e-jhul*) used together 41 with a breast cover (*sīna-band*, *galla-band*, or *gardan-band*) that serve more as 42 a protection for the animal during cold weather than as trappings.

3. A cover for cattle (*gŏk-e-jhul*) was, because of the width required, made up of two loom widths. The two pieces were left unstitched at the front for a length of 30–40 cm.; this slit allowed the hump of the bull to project. A cord kept the two corners together in front of the hump. A second cord, attached to one front edge and passed through a loop on the opposite edge below the breast, held the cover and prevented it slipping. This luxurious article has now disappeared. When cattle breeders in the eastern part of the country exhibit their bulls at festivals and *mēlas*, they now use the Sindhi patchwork blankets.

4. An ornamental cover for greyhounds (*tāzī-e-jhul*) is a small piece between 43 50–70 cm. square which was fastened over the chest of the animal with a cord fixed to one side close to the front edge of the cover, and passed through a loop on the opposite side. This cover has also disappeared, mainly on account of a considerable decrease in wild life. Hunters who keep greyhounds today are rare, and prices for dogs vary between 1000–2000 Rs. For the protection of their pets they now use the cheaper felt or even rough hessian cloth.

Other textiles made and used by the Baluchis are cradle cloths and prayer rugs. The cradle cloth (*julūnt*) is roughly square and has strong plaited cords 47 with tassels at each corner by means of which it is suspended from a special stand.

The prayer rug (*sajjāda*) seems to have been woven very seldom. I did not 48 see it in central Baluchistan, where the men's multipurpose cotton shawl (*chādar*) or a mat made from dwarf palm leaves were used for praying. Only recently have I seen two prayer rugs woven by Baluchis (Mahērī) in Sind (Sind Provincial Museum, Hyderabad, Pakistan). A specimen from Farah, Afghanistan, is illustrated in Plate 48.

Baluchi flat weave textiles in Sind and Derajat

Whenever people change from nomadic life to a settled existence certain of their material possessions cease to be essential and are discarded. This development can be observed in the case of all Baluchi tribes who migrated to Sind at least two centuries ago. The use of one object, however, the floor cover, has persisted in three forms.

1. A floor cover with stripes in various shades. The warp is often goat hair and the weft sheep's wool and/or camel hair. This article is called *kharrarī*, the equivalent of the *garrag* of Baluchistan.

2. A floor cover designed in the traditional manner for a floor or bed cover (*kōnt* or *katpōsh*). For the warp, camel hair or cotton are used; for the weft sheep's wool, camel hair and bleached cotton (for white). This article is called *farasī*.

3. A floor cover in which the arrangement of the design is like that on ornamental covers for animals (*jhul*), woven with the same materials as 2 and also called *farasī*.

None of the three types generally exceeds 120×200 cm. in size. The fibres of the brown shades of these weaves, generally stated to be camel hair, are often the wool of a particular breed of sheep.

The name of the last mentioned type indicates its use as a floor cover (Persian: *farsh* = floor carpet), and the word may have been introduced by Persian carpet weavers who settled in Bubak (Sind) during the last period of Mughul rule. The *farasī* does not serve as a floor cover only, it is also commonly used as a bedspread. It is, therefore, not surprising that its prototype in design is the classic *kōnt* and *katpōsh*. Less easy to explain, however, is the inclusion of *jhul* (animal cover) designs with their various geometric motifs. Since most of the ornamental covers for animals in flat weave technique have disappeared in central Baluchistan, this type of *farasī* can be considered evidence of the many variations of design which once existed in this type of woven article.

The basic arrangements of motifs in the panel are sometimes similar to that of a medallion rug, with the placing of a square (in place of the medallion) in the centre, and one quarter of the square motif in each corner. I have seen very interesting examples in the possession of elderly people (who sometimes call them *jhul*) who enjoy their beauty and try to keep them as long as possible by repairing them with leather patches until they fall to pieces.

Since designs originating in two different covers (*kōnt* and *jhul*) are clearly used in the *farasī*, they can be called *kōnt-farasī* and *jhul-farasī*.

The *farasīs* which are woven today with thick yarn show a distortion of patterns and unpleasant colour combinations. These articles have recently and on various occasions been referred to as 'Sindhi' carpets (Qadiri, 1966, p. 34), but since they are undeniably produced by Baluchis (Aitken, 1907, p. 392), according to traditional Baluchi layout, and employing Baluchi patterns, they should be classified as Baluchi.

The horse nose-bags still produced by Baluchis in Sind (as horse breeding continues in that area) differ from those once use in central Baluchistan in their shape and style of decoration. The bottom fold is wider than the opening which is achieved by tapering the sides. The colour is generally white with a broad patterned band running horizontally around the upper half.

An entirely different style of design is used on textiles from Derajat. The main panel as well as the borders are symmetrical. The pattern stripes are, moreover, usually filled with motifs which are not known in central Baluchistan. These were probably introduced by (male) weavers whose ancestors are said to have come from Afghanistan.

Plate 1
Bedding cover (*shaffi*), Zaggar
Mengal tribe, Nushki, Chagai,
Baluchistan, Pakistan, and other
Baluchi tribes living on both sides
of the Pakistan-Afghanistan border.
360 × 105 cm.
1970 AS21 7

Black, purple, red and green
striped ground with red and white
patterns. Weft faced plain weave
with pattern wefts floating on the
reverse. All wool.

Plate 2
Bedding cover (*shafft*), Zaggar
Mengal tribe, Nushki, Chagai,
Baluchistan, Pakistan, and other
Baluchi tribes living on both sides
of the Pakistan-Afghanistan
border.
361 × 124 cm.
1970 AS21 8

Green, dark red and light red
banded ground with patterns in
white. All wool, with a string
sewn along one edge with goat
hair for strength. Weft faced plain
weave with pattern wefts floating
on the reverse.

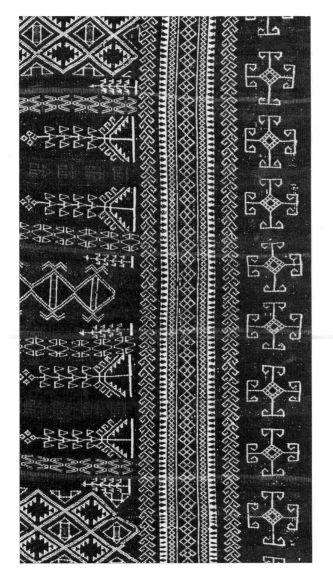

Plate 3
Jangi Khan sitting in his tent.
Killi Mengal, Chagai, Pakistan.
In the background can be seen
the bedding pile with a bedding
cover (*shaffi*) draped over part of
it. The upper part of the bedding
cover is covered with a runner
(*mon phul*) of red and green silk
patchwork decorated with white
shells, buttons and tassels.

Plate 4
Floor cover (*kōnt*), Kharan,
Baluchistan, Pakistan.
236 × 104 cm.
1970 AS21 1

Black goat hair ground with
patterns in white goat hair.
Weft faced plain weave with
pattern wefts floating on the
reverse.
Used as a floor cover by people
too poor to afford more elaborate
rugs.

Plate 5
Floor cover (*kōnt*), Baluchi tribes,
Shorawak, Kandahar, Afghanistan
(see colour plate 13).
256 × 131 cm.
1970 AS21 9

Red, brown and blue banded
ground with patterns in white,
red and blue. Weft faced plain
weave with pattern wefts floating
on the reverse. All wool.

Plate 6
Floor cover (*kōnt*), Baluchi tribes,
Nimroz (Chakhansur), Afghanistan.
296 × 168 cm.
1970 AS21 2

Black, purple, red and green
banded ground, patterns in white
and a little red. Weft faced plain
weave with pattern wefts floating
on the reverse. Two widths joined
lengthways. All wool with goat-
hair stitching.

Plate 7
Floor cover (*kōnt*), Reki tribe,
Zaranj, Nimroz, Afghanistan.
160 × 100 cm.
1973 AS7 5

Beige, purple, brown, orange and
black stripes and bands. Patterns
in beige and orange slit tapestry.
Weft faced plain weave.
Embroidered border patterns in
orange. Small transverse patterns
in white with weft floating on the
reverse. Tufts of wool inserted at
intervals. All wool.

Plate 8
Floor cover (*kōnt*), Bangulzai
tribe, Isplinji, Sarawan,
Baluchistan, Pakistan (see Cover).
240 × 108 cm.
1970 AS21 6

Brown, beige, red, blue and green
ground with patterns in the same
colours and white. The patterns
include a row of camels. Weft
faced plain weave with pattern
wefts floating on the reverse.

Plate 9
Floor cover (*kŏnt* or *katpōsh*),
Samulari tribe, Mastung,
Baluchistan, Pakistan.
193 × 94 cm.
1970 AS21 5

Red ground with patterns in blue,
white and pink. All wool. Weft
faced plain weave with pattern
wefts floating on the reverse.
This piece may have been
intended originally as a bedding
cover (*shaffi*) as it has at one end
short sections of pattern bands
(*harīr*) typical of bedding covers.

Plate 10
Floor cover (*farasī*), Lerwani
(Rind) tribe, Kakrand, Mirpur
Sakro, Sind, Pakistan (see colour
plate 20).
214 × 114 cm.
1970 AS21 4

Red, brown, blue and white
striped and banded ground, with
patterns in the same colours.
All wool. Weft faced plain weave
with pattern wefts floating on the
reverse. Strings sewn along the
selvedges for strength.

Plate 11
Meal cloth (*parzōnag*), Rakhshani
or Reki tribe, Nimroz (Chakhansur), Afghanistan, or Janbegi
tribe, Khaf, Khorasan, Iran.
114 × 63 cm.
1973 AS7 3

Orange, dark brown, light brown
and blue areas with small
patterns in orange and white.
Dovetailed or interlocked tapestry
weave with the wefts of the small
patterns floating on the reverse.
All wool.

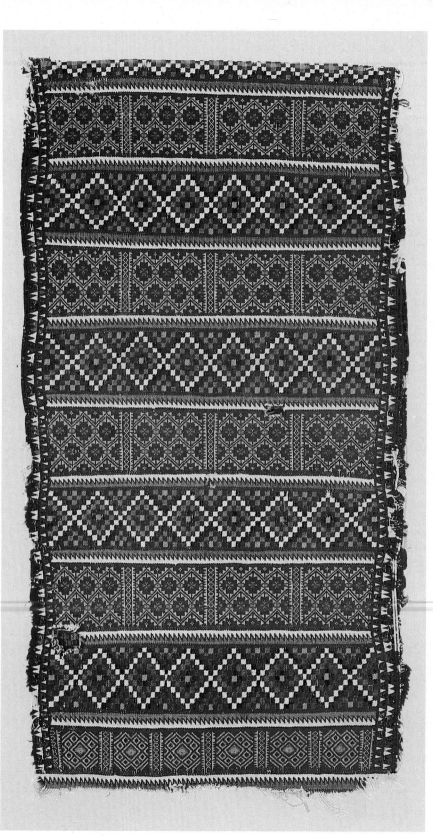

Plate 12
Storage bag (*takkī*), Maheri tribe,
Kario Ganwhar, Sind, Pakistan.
184 × 48 cm.
1970 AS21 15

Wefts in red, blue, green and
yellow wool and white cotton,
cotton warp. Weft faced plain
weave, more complex pattern
bands having wefts floating on
the reverse.

Plate 13
Detail of floor cover, Shorawak,
Kandahar, Afghanistan (see plate 5).

Plates 14, 15

Left Decoration (*shishajel*) for the
forelegs of a camel. Used at
weddings. Kethrani tribe, Dera
Ismail Khan, Pakistan.
Right Camel necklace (*gorband*).
Southern Afghanistan and Chagai
district, Pakistan (see plate 45).
Lengths 55 cm. and 68 cm.
1973 AS7 10 and 14

Plate 16

Detail from a salt bag, Dalbandin, .
Pakistan (see plate 32).

Plate 17
Floor cover (*zīl, kōnt*), Angaria
tribe, Haro range, Las Bela,
Baluchistan, Pakistan.
256 × 148 cm.
1970 AS21 3

Plates 18, 19
Storage bags/cushions (*takkī*),
Sanjrani tribe, Chagai,
Baluchistan, Pakistan.
94 × 58 cm. and 94 × 62 cm.
1970 AS21 13 and 14

Red, orange, green, white and
black banded and striped ground
with patterns in the same colours.
Weft faced plain weave with
pattern wefts floating on the
reverse.

Red ground with white, black,
green and yellow patterns. Wool
with goat-hair stitching and loops.
Weft faced plain weave with
pattern wefts floating on the
reverse.

Plate 20
Detail from a floor cover, Sind,
Pakistan (see plate 10).

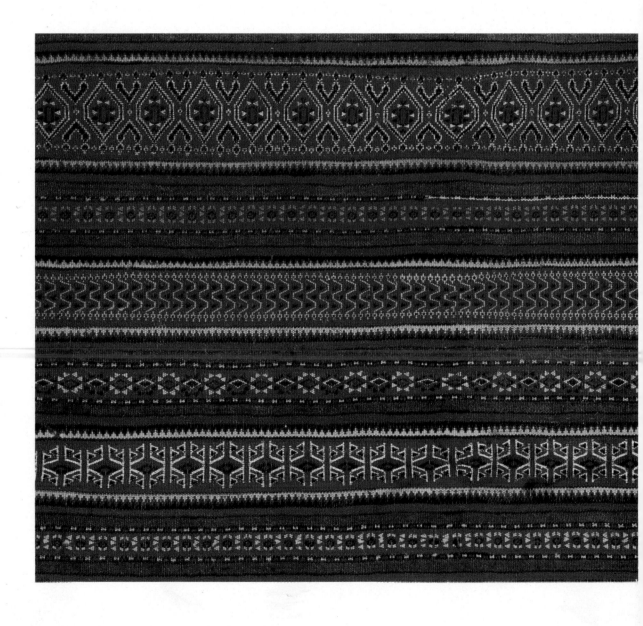

Plate 21

Floor cover (kōnt or plas),
Kethrani tribe, Barkhan, Dera
Ismail Khan, Pakistan.
188 × 116 cm.
1973 AS7 6

Purple, dark pink, orange and
brown wool ground. Patterns in
the same colours and white
cotton. Weft faced plain weave
with pattern wefts floating on the
reverse. The patterns are arranged
symmetrically lengthways and
widthways. The latter is unusual
in Baluch flat woven textiles. The
patterned borders are similar to
those found on bedding covers.
This tribe is unusual in that its
weavers are all men.

Plate 22
Floor cover (*jhul-farasī*), Lerwani
tribe, Kakrand, Mirpur Sakro,
Sind, Pakistan.
237 × 116 cm.
1973 AS7 7

Dark red, light red and blue
striped and banded ground with
patterns in white, blue and red.
Weft faced plain weave with
pattern wefts floating on the
reverse.

Plate 23
Dough and bread bag (*shēken*),
Rakhshani tribe, Chagai,
Baluchistan, Pakistan.
280 (140 doubled) × 82 cm.
1970 AS21 22

Plate 24
Flour bags (*gowālag*), Rakhshani
tribe, Chagai, Baluchistan,
Pakistan.
45 × 30 cm. and 80 × 44 cm.
1970 AS21 19 and 20

White wool ground with patterns
in black goat hair. Weft faced
plain weave with pattern wefts
floating on the reverse. (The bag
is illustrated doubled although it
has not been joined at the sides.)

Left White wool ground with
patterns in red wool and black
goat hair. Weft faced plain weave
with pattern wefts floating on
the reverse.
Right White wool ground with
patterns in red and green wool
and black goat hair. Weft faced
plain weave with pattern wefts
floating on the reverse. Used to
store and transport flour and
grain.

Plate 25
Runner (*dasdān*), Baluchi tribes,
Chagai, Baluchistan, Pakistan.
180 × 33 cm.
1970 AS21 11

Red and green banded ground
with green, red and white
patterns. Weft faced plain weave
with pattern wefts floating on
reverse. All wool. One long edge
is often decorated with shells and
tassels.

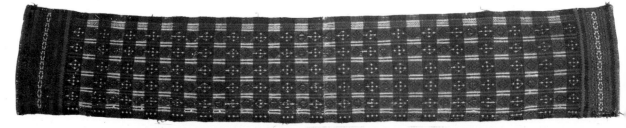

Plate 26
Bag (*jamdān*) kept on top of
bedding cover, Baluchi tribes,
Chagai, Baluchistan, Afghanistan.
90 × 33 cm.
1970 AS21 10

All-over pink, orange, green and
white patterns. Weft faced plain
weave with pattern wefts floating
on the reverse. Goat-hair stitching
and loops. Shells sewn along one
edge. New pieces usually also have
tassels along the lower edge.

Plate 27
Saddle-bag (*hōrjīn*), Baluchi tribes,
Khorasan (Iran) or Herat
(Afghanistan).
120 × 44 cm.
1973 AS7 1

Red, purple, blue, brown and
white wool. Some white wool is
mixed with metal thread. Loops
and stitching of goat hair. Weft
faced plain weave with pattern
wefts floating on the reverse.
Lines of soumak(?) weave
between main pattern bands.
Back of bag in cream plain weave.

Plate 28
Saddle-bag (*hōrjīn*), Mamassani
(Muhammad Hassani) tribe,
Pamile, Baluchistan, Iran.
155 × 71 cm.
1970 AS21 16

Red, green, blue and white wool.
Back: brown and red stripes.
Face: all-over Soumak brocading
with slit tapestry panels at
opening. Back weft-faced plain
weave. Edging, loops and tassel
of goat hair. Decorated along one
edge with three species of shells
and blue ceramic beads.

Plate 29
Saddle-bag (*hōrjīn*), Baluchi tribes,
western Afghanistan.
93 × 42 cm.
1970 AS21 17

Plate 30
Koran bag (*Qur'ān jal*), Zaggar
Mengal tribe, Nushki, Chagai,
Baluchistan, Pakistan.
43 × 37 cm.
1970 AS21 24

Brown, white and blue wool with
goat-hair stitching. Weft faced
plain weave with pattern wefts
floating on the reverse. Back:
dark brown, light brown and blue
bands with white patterns.

Purple ground with red, green and
white patterns. Weft faced plain
weave with pattern wefts floating
on the reverse. Purple and green
tassels with decorative cotton
bindings and shell ornaments.
All wool.

Plate 31
Salt bag (*wādān*), Zaggar Mengal
tribe, Nushki, Chagai, Baluchistan,
Pakistan.
51 × 35 cm.
1970 AS21 23a

Plate 32
Salt bag (*wādān*), Sanjrani tribe,
Dalbandin, Chagai, Baluchistan,
Pakistan (see colour plate 16).
56 × 38 cm.
1970 AS21 23b

Red ground with patterns in
white, green and orange. Tassels
in green, red and black, decorated
with multi-coloured cotton
bindings and bone and shell
ornaments. All wool. Weft faced
plain weave with pattern wefts
floating on the reverse.

White ground with patterns in
red, green and yellow. All wool.
Weft faced plain weave with
pattern wefts floating on the
reverse.

Plate 33
Vanity bag (*istrajal*), Sanjrani
tribe, Dalbandin, Chagai,
Pakistan.
33 × 32 cm.
IC 44 135
(Museum für Völkerkunde, Berlin)

Red, yellow, blue and white.
Weft faced plain weave with
pattern wefts floating on the
reverse. All wool. Decorated with
shells.

Plate 34
Vanity bag (*istrajal*), Baluchi
tribes, Nimroz (Chakhansur),
Afghanistan.
30 × 28 cm.
1970 AS21 26

Red, purple, white and black
patterned bag. Weft faced plain
weave with pattern wefts floating
on the reverse. All wool. The
tassels are of the same coloured
wools with decorative woollen
bindings and shell ornaments.
Wool with goat-hair loops.

61

Plate 35
Vanity·bag (*khīsajal*), Chakarzai
(Reki) tribe, Nimroz (Chakhansur), Afghanistan.
39 × 36 cm.
1975 AS6 1

Red, dark blue and white
patterned bag. Weft faced plain
weave with pattern wefts floating
on the reverse. Tassels in the
same colours ornamented with
shells. Wool with goat-hair loops.

Plate 36
Vanity bag (*istrajal*), Rakhshani
tribe, Nimroz (Chakhansur),
Afghanistan.
36 × 36 cm.
1974 AS7 1

Brown and white ground with
patterns in brown and red. Weft
faced plain weave with pattern
wefts floating on the reverse.
Pattern sections outlined by
twined wefts. All wool. The
animal figures represent antelopes.

Plate 37
Horse-shoe bag (*nāldān*), Mengal
(Brahui) tribes, Chagai or
Sarawan, Baluchistan, Pakistan.
26 × 24 cm.
1970 AS21 27

Plate 38
Horse nose-bag (*tūrag*), Zaggar
Mengal tribe, Killi Mengal, Chagai,
Pakistan.
43 × 39 cm.
IC 44 144
(Museum für Völkerkunde, Berlin)

Red ground with yellow, white,
blue and green patterns. All wool.
Originally ornamented with tassels
which are now missing.

Red, yellow, blue, green and
white. Plain weave with pattern
wefts floating on the reverse. All
cotton including tassels.
Decorated with shells. This item is
unusual in being made entirely
from cotton, yet coming from an
area where cotton is not grown
at all.

Plate 39
Camel saddle-cloth (*ushter-e-jhul*),
Jamaldini tribe, Jamaldini Killi,
Nushki, Chagai, Baluchistan,
Pakistan.
137 × 96 cm.
1970 AS21 12

Plate 40
Camel decorated for a festive
occasion, wearing a head-piece,
necklaces, knee pads and a saddle
cover. Killi Mengal, Chagai,
Pakistan.

Purple and brown wool ground
with patterns in white, orange
and brown wool. Weft faced plain
weave with pattern wefts floating on the reverse. Edging in red
and green twined(?) weave. White
woollen warp left as fringe at two
ends. Originally this piece had three
large tassels on each long side.

Plate 41
Horse saddle cover (*asp-e jhul*),
Zaggar Mengal tribe, Killi Mengal,
Chagai, Pakistan.
145 × 120 cm.
IC 44 138A
(Museum für Völkerkunde, Berlin)

Plate 42
Chest cover (*sīna band*) for a horse,
Zaggar Mengal tribe, Killi Mengal,
Chagai, Pakistan.
80 × 40 cm.
IC 44 138B
(Museum für Völkerkunde, Berlin)

Maroon, red, orange, blue, black
and white. Plain weave with
pattern wefts floating on the
reverse. All wool.

Maroon, red, blue, green, black
and white. Weft faced plain
weave with pattern wefts floating
on the reverse. All wool.

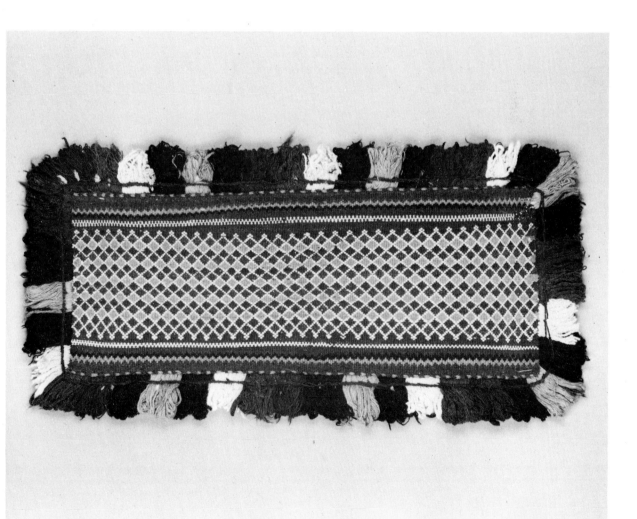

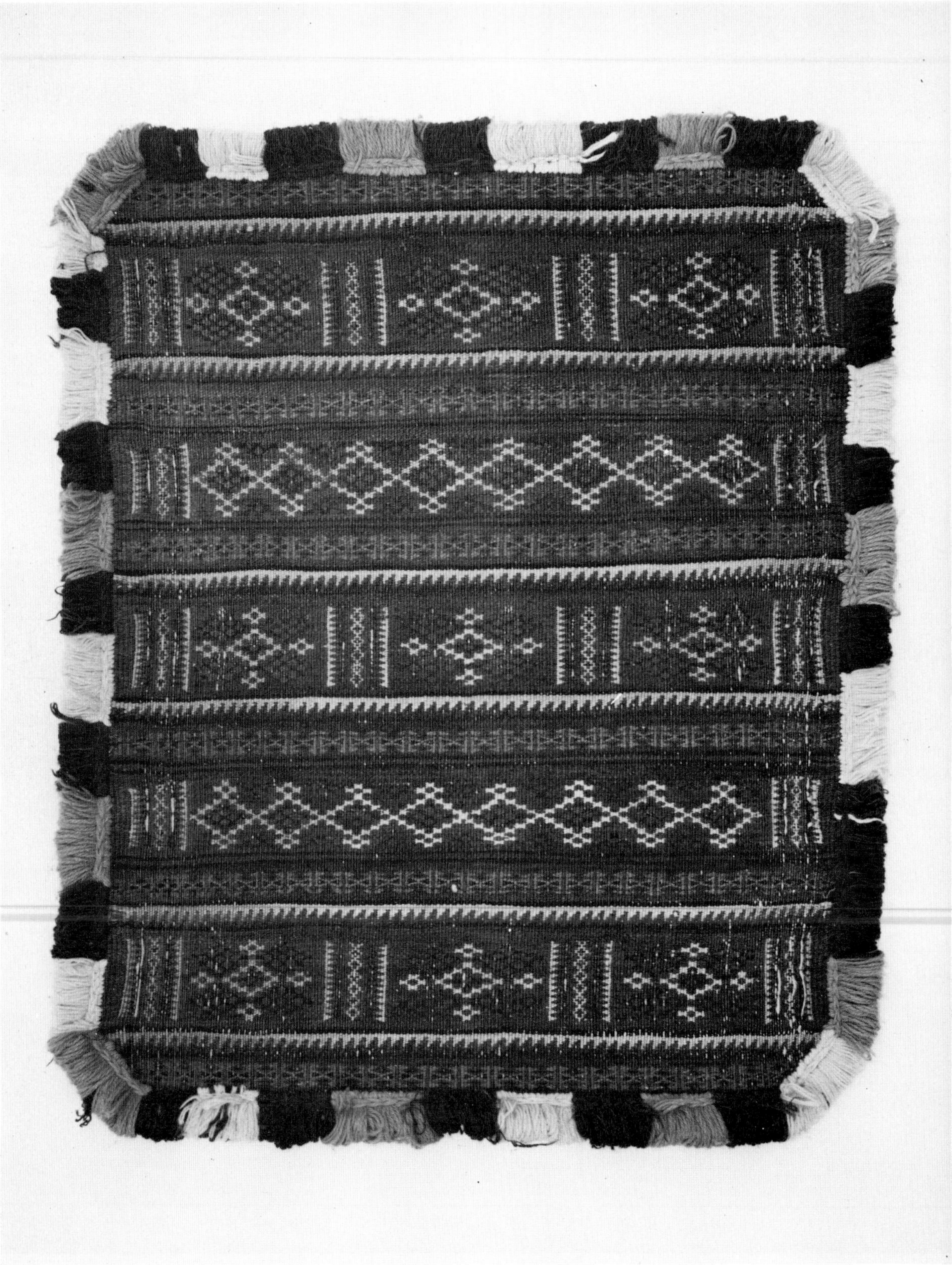

Plate 43
Greyhound cover (*tāzī-e-jhul*),
Zaggar Mengal tribe, Chagai and
Mengal tribes in Sarawan,
Baluchistan, Pakistan.
74 × 61 cm.
1975 AS6 2

Plate 44
Camel collar (*gardan-band*),
Janbegi tribe, Khorasan, Iran.
117 cm.
1973 AS7 15

Orange, red, white and green
wool. Weft faced plain weave with
pattern wefts floating on the
reverse.

Red, blue, brown and white wool
with brown goat-hair borders.
Soumak brocading for patterned
panel in the centre, plain weave
borders and floating weft patterns
in a band at each end.

Plate 45
Camel necklaces (*gutti* or
gorband), Baluchi tribes on both
sides of the Afghanistan-Pakistan
border, Nimroz, Girishk and
Chagai (see colour plate 15).
80 cm. and 68 cm. (lengths)
1972 AS2 53 and 1973 AS 7 14

Bands of plaited goat hair with
appliqué silk and cotton fabrics.
Left: tassels in red, yellow and
green wool. Right: tassels in red,
orange, green, brown and purple
silk and wool with some black
goat hair. Both with ornamental
tassel tops, and shells and (left)
buttons for decoration.

Plate 46
Net bag (*tasdān*) for storing dishes,
Baluchi tribes on both sides of the
Afghanistan-Pakistan border,
Nimroz, Girishk and Chagai.
250 cm. (length)
1972 AS2 51

Plaited goat hair with green,
brown, red and orange wool
tassels.

73

Plate 47
Cradle (*julūnt*), Zaggar Mengal
tribe, Killi Mengal, Chagai,
Baluchistan, Pakistan.
57 × 56 cm.
1973 AS7 2(a)

Plate 48
Prayer rug (*sajjādā*), Baluch,
Farah, Afghanistan.
73 × 57 cm.
1974 AS2 37

Purple, red, orange, green and
white wool. Weft faced plain
weave with pattern wefts floating
on the reverse. Tassels in the same
coloured wools and brown, with
shell ornaments.
The cradle is shown flat and also
suspended from its stand as it
would be in the tent.

White wool plain weave ground
with weft-float brocading in red,
orange, purple, black and blue
wool.

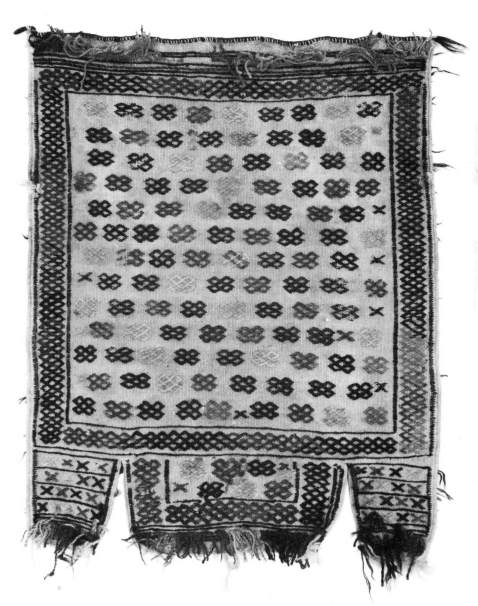

Select Bibliography

B.D.G.S. =
Baluchistan District Gazetteer Series

AITKEN, E. H. 1907
Gazetteer of the Province of Sind. Karachi,
Mercantile Press.
(On Baluch weavings in Sind.)

GUPTE, B. A. 1907a
Memorandum on weaving (with technical terms in Pushtu) and notes on
dyeing. *B.D.G.S.*, Vol. I (Zhob),
ed. C. F. Minchin.
Bombay, Education Society's Press.

GUPTE, B. A. 1907b
Memorandum on weaving (with technical terms in Pushtu) and notes on
dyeing. *B.D.G.S.*, Vol. V (Quetta/ Pishin),
ed. R. Hughes-Buller. Ajmer,
Scottish Mission Industries Co. Ltd.

GUPTE, B. A. 1907c
Memorandum on weaving (with technical terms in Baluchi) and notes on
dyeing. *B.D.G.S.*, Vol. VIB (Jhalawan),
ed. C. F. Minchin. Bombay,
Education Society's Press.

HUGHES, T. O. 1907
Notes on weaving and dyeing. *B.D.G.S.*,
Vol. IV A (Chagai), ed. A. McConnaghey.
Bombay, The Mercantile Press.

KIPLING, J. LOCKWOOD. 1898
Weaving industry of the Derajat Hills.
*Gazetteer of the Dera Ghazi Khan District
1893–97* (Punjab Gazetteer,
revised edition 1898). Lahore.

KIPLING, J. LOCKWOOD. 1902
Memorandum on weaving. *Gazetteer of
the Multan District 1901–02*,
ed. E. D. Maclagan. Lahore, Civil and
Military Gazette Press.

LATIMER, COURTHENAY. 1907
*Monograph on carpet making in the
Punjab 1905–06.* Lahore: 19. (Note on
Baluch weavings.)

McCONNAGHEY, A. 1907
Cultivation of indigo. *B.D.G.S.*, Vol. III
(Sibi). Bombay, The Times Press.

MASSON, CHARLES. 1844
*Narrative of various journeys in
Baluchistan, Afghanistan, the Punjab and
Kalat*, Vol. IV. London, Richard Bentley.

MINCHIN, C. F. 1907a
Cultivation of madder and notes on
dyeing. *B.D.G.S.*, Vol. VI (Sarawan).
Bombay, The Times Press.

MINCHIN, C. F. 1907b
Cultivation of indigo. *B.D.G.S.*, Vol. VIA
(Kachhi). Bombay, The Times Press.

MINCHIN, C. F. 1907c
The mordant *mak* (*phulmak, khaghal* or
zagh). *B.D.G.S.*, Vol. VIB (Jhalawan).
Bombay, Bombay Education Society's
Press.

MINCHIN, C. F. 1907d
Dyeing wool. *B.D.G.S.*, Vol. VIIA
(Kharan). Bombay, The Times Press.

MINCHIN, C. F. 1907e
B.D.G.S., Vol. VIII (Las Bela). Allahabad,
The Pioneer Press. (Description of an
Angaria floor cover with illustration.)

MORRIS, C. 1884
Cultivation and manufacture of indigo.
Gazetteer of the Mooltan District 1883–84,
App. A. Lahore, Arya Press.

QADIRI, MADAD ALI. 1966
*The traditional arts and crafts of
Hyderabad region*, ed. N. A. Baloch.
Hyderabad. (On textiles in Sind.)

TATE, G. P. 1909
The frontiers of Baluchistan. London:
Witherby & Co. (On weaving in Seistan.)

ZICK-NISSEN, JOHANNA, 1968
Nomadenkunst aus Baluchistan. Berlin,
Kunstamt Reinickendorf. (Catalogue of
an exhibition of Baluch textiles.)